STO

FRIENDS
OF ACPL

P9-CLD-347

3 1833 02066 2240

j508.315
Barrett, Norman S.
Deserts

DO NOT REMOVE
CARDS FROM POCKET

ALLEN COUNTY PUBLIC LIBRARY

FORT WAYNE, INDIANA 46802

You may return this book to any agency, branch,
or bookmobile of the Allen County Public Library

DEMCO

PICTURE LIBRARY

DESERTS

PICTURE LIBRARY
DESERTS

Norman Barrett

Franklin Watts

London   New York   Sydney   Toronto

Allen County Public Library
Ft. Wayne, Indiana

© 1989 Franklin Watts

First published in the USA by
Franklin Watts Inc
387 Park Avenue South
New York
NY 10016

US ISBN: 0-531-10
Library of Congress Catalog Card
Number 8 –

Printed in Italy

Designed by
Barrett and Weintroub

Photographs by
Arizona Office of Tourism
Australian Overseas Information Service, London
GeoScience Features
Peter Rabin
Remote Source
Royal Geographical Society
Satour
South American Pictures
Survival Anglia
Xinhua News Agency

Illustration by
Rhoda and Robert Burns

Technical Consultant
Keith Lye

Contents

Introduction

Deserts are regions of land where little or no rain falls and the ground is dry nearly all the time. They can be sandy, stony or covered by bare rock. Deserts may consist of dry, dusty soil.

△ The sands of the Sahara, the world's largest desert. The wind blows the sand into low hills called dunes.

Most desert lands lie in hot regions. But there are also cold deserts, and even the hottest deserts can be very cold at night. Some people regard the polar lands as deserts, because the air is dry and little rain falls.

Little grows in desert lands, although they are not completely barren. Some desert plants get water from deep beneath the surface.

Animals, too, have found ways to live in arid (dry) regions. Desert animals include insects, reptiles, birds and mammals.

Few people live in desert lands. Those that do have learned how to adjust to the hot, dry climate.

△ People who live in some desert regions use camels as a means of transportation. The camel can go longer without food and water than any other domesticated animal.

Looking at deserts

Major deserts of the world

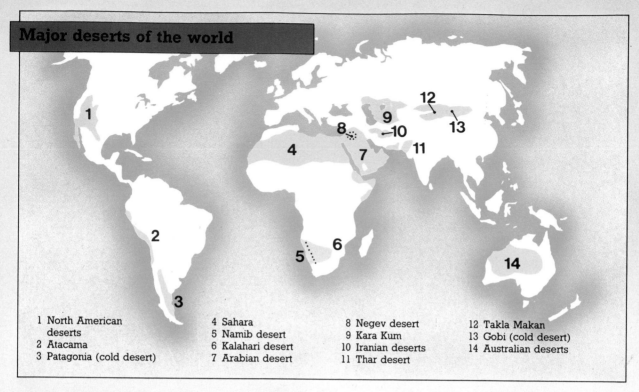

1 North American deserts	4 Sahara	8 Negev desert	12 Takla Makan
2 Atacama	5 Namib desert	9 Kara Kum	13 Gobi (cold desert)
3 Patagonia (cold desert)	6 Kalahari desert	10 Iranian deserts	14 Australian deserts
	7 Arabian desert	11 Thar desert	

Water in the desert

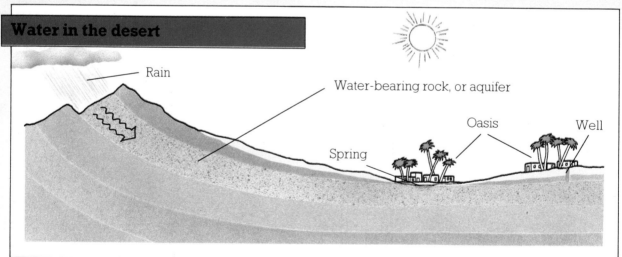

Rain · Water-bearing rock, or aquifer · Spring · Oasis · Well

Under some deserts there are rock layers, called aquifers, containing water that seeps through the rock. The water might have come from rain that fell hundreds of miles away. If the aquifer is near the surface, a well may be dug down to it. Or a break in the rock might force the water to the surface as a spring. Water also comes to the surface if an aquifer is exposed. Oases grow up around water that can come to the surface.

8

Rain shadow

Moist winds (blue) from the ocean change to dry winds (red) after crossing a range of mountains. The dry region on the other side of the mountains is called a rain shadow.

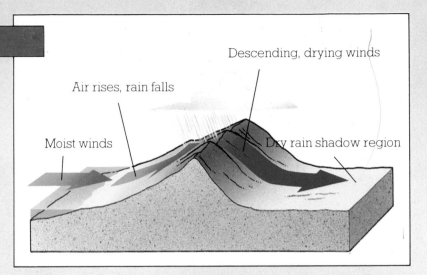

Descending, drying winds

Air rises, rain falls

Moist winds

Dry rain shadow region

Prevailing wind

Formation of dunes

The simplest sand dunes are called barchans. They form when there is a prevailing, or main, wind blowing most of the time. They are crescent-shaped.

Erosion

The wearing away of rock by the action of wind and water is called erosion. Soft rocks are worn away first. In rocky deserts that take the form of a plateau (a high, flat region), the rock may be eroded unevenly, leaving mesas and buttes.

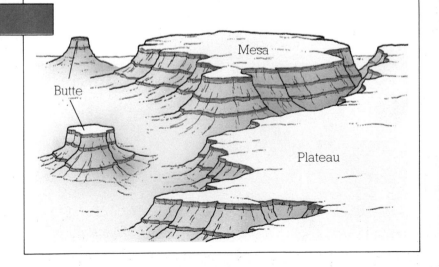

Mesa

Butte

Plateau

Kinds of deserts

Most people think of deserts as vast expanses of sand. But only about a fifth of the world's hot desert area are sandy. The rest consist chiefly of stones, rocks, mountains or various types of dry soil.

Sand consists of loose grains of solid rocks that have crumbled away. In desert areas, wind-blown sand wears away the rock. In some areas winds blow the sand away leaving only bare rock.

△ Sand dunes in the Thar desert of northwestern India. Sandy deserts are known as erg, their Arabic name.

▷ A rocky part of the Negev desert, in southern Israel. Rocky deserts are called hammada.

▽ Parts of the Atacama desert, in Chile, are stony. Stony deserts are known as reg.

◁ Dunes of the Wahiba Sands, in Oman, on the Arabian peninsula.

Dunes are caused by the wind. They are like waves in the sea, but they form much more slowly.

There are several kinds of dunes, formed by the wind. Regular winds cause the sand to pile up in crescentshaped dunes called barchans. Seif dunes are long ridges of sand that form in the direction of the main, or prevailing wind. Other winds blowing at rightangles to the prevailing wind curve the sides of the ridges. When winds blow from all directions, the sand dunes are shapeless.

Sand dunes move slowly as the wind pushes the sand forward, perhaps 10 m (33 ft) a year. They sometimes reach great heights, and whole villages or even cities have been buried underneath them.

Living in the desert

Deserts cannot support large populations. But peoples in many parts of the world have adapted to living in deserts.

The Bushmen of the Kalahari, in Africa, and the Aborigines of Australia are hunter-gatherers. They live on roots and other plant food gathered mainly by the women, and on small animals caught by the men. They know where water can be found under the ground.

▽ An encampment of Baluchi nomads in the Dasht-e-Lut desert of Iran. They wander the desert with their flocks of sheep and goats. They set up camp in their black tents made of goat hair wherever they find grazing land for their animals.

In some places people live at oases, places in the desert where there is water.

Small towns and villages have grown up around many oases. The people keep farm animals such as cattle and goats, and grow crops such as dates and olives.

Farmers who wander the deserts are called nomads. They travel from oasis to oasis with their sheep and goats. They use camels and donkeys to carry their tents and other possessions.

△ A group of desert nomads with their camels and donkeys by the pyramids of Giza, near Cairo, in Egypt.

15

▷ An oasis village in the Iranian desert. Irrigation water comes from deep wells.

◁ Scientists use an anemometer (wind gauge) to study how winds shape sand dunes. A local Bedouin tribesman can provide valuable information about how the dunes have changed over many years.

▽ Earthmoving machines dig out a huge hole in the Australian desert. This will serve as a reservoir to catch and store rainwater.

Animal life

Wild animals that live in deserts usually feed at night when it is cooler. In the daytime, the larger animals try to keep in the shade Many smaller animals dig burrows under the ground and stay in them during the day.

Reptiles, like snakes and lizards, that live in hot deserts can stand more heat than the mammals. Their waterproof skin helps them to keep their body moisture.

△ Gemsbok are antelopes that live in the Kalahari desert in southern Africa. They can survive long spells of drought.

18

▷ The sidewinder is a rattlesnake. It moves with a sideways motion that makes the minimum of contact with the hot ground.

▽ The kangaroo rat nests in burrows or under rocks during the day. It gets all the water it needs from plant food.

Most desert animals can go for several days without water. Many do not drink water. They get all the water they need from plants and other food, like insects.

Desert birds obtain their water from the seeds or insects they eat, or they may visit oases. They can travel long distances in search of water if necessary.

▽ The scorpion is one of the most common animals found living in the desert. It hunts mainly at night, using the deadly sting at the end of its tail to kill its prey. It lives on insects and spiders, but can go for long periods without any food.

△ The bearded dragon is a large lizard of the Australian deserts. Lizards are found in most deserts. They are the most successful animal group to adapt to the dry desert conditions.

◁ The gila woodpecker lives in the deserts of the southwestern United States. It pecks out the soft flesh of the saguaro and other giant cactus plants to make a nesting hole.

Plant life

Few plants grow in deserts during dry periods. Some have long roots and get water from deep underground. Others store water in their roots or in their leaves or stems.

Many desert plants do not grow when it is dry. When it rains, they suddenly sprout up. They may flower within a few weeks. But they scatter their seeds before they die, and the process begins again the next time it rains.

▷ An organ-pipe cactus in the Sonoran desert of the southwestern United States. Cactus plants store large amounts of water when it rains. Some have deep roots that make use of underground water.

▽ Sudden heavy rain after 50 years of drought produced a remarkable rate of growth in this desert flower – 36 cm (14 in) in 10 hours.

◁ Plants often burst into life after desert rains. These red flowers sprang up in Chile's Atacama desert, one of the driest places in the world.

Parts of the desert have not had any rain in our time. But rainfall there is sudden, quick and very heavy. The desert soon dries out, but the flowers last for a few weeks, in the cracked, baked mud. Their seeds will then lie dormant until the next rainfall, perhaps in hundreds of years' time.

25

Riches under the desert

Some deserts are rich in oil or minerals, including precious metals and stones. When oil was discovered under the deserts of the Middle East, land that had been regarded as useless suddenly became valuable.

Metals such as gold and copper are mined or quarried from desert lands in many parts of the world. Diamonds and other precious stones are also found, as well as the raw materials used for nuclear fuels.

△ A copper mine in Chile. The northern part of the desert, which covers a third of Chile's area, contains its greatest wealth. Many other minerals are also mined there.

▷ A test drilling rig in the Takla Makan desert of northwestern China will determine whether there are oil riches under the shifting sand dunes.

The story of deserts

How deserts form

Dry conditions on earth are caused by movements of air. Warm air rising at the equator cools, and drops its moisture in the form of rain. The air spreads out north and south. As the dry air moves farther away from the equator, it cools and finally sinks down. Most deserts lie in zones of the earth where this cool, dry air sinks. As it sinks, it becomes warm. Warm air can hold more moisture than cold air, so it absorbs any moisture and creates the dry conditions in which deserts form.

Some deserts have formed in areas separated from an ocean by mountains. Clouds laden with moisture from the ocean lose it as they move over the mountains. The air then becomes hot and dry as it flows down the far side.

Coastal deserts, such as the Atacama in Chile, have formed because the winds are chilled by cold currents in the oceans. The cold air starts to warm up when it blows over the land. As it warms, it picks up moisture, causing deserts.

△ King Solomon's Pillars, in the south of the Negev desert, in Israel, an area that has changed little since Biblical times.

△ The bleak and dry Death Valley, in California. The western deserts of the United States are a good example of how moisture from the ocean falls on the windward side of mountains, so that the winds are dry when they have crossed the mountains and this creates desert conditions.

Sandy deserts

Only a small part of the world's deserts are sandy. Sand is made up of small particles of rock. It forms over millions of years as rock crumbles from constant weathering by the wind or water. The sand is then blown away, perhaps into a corner of the desert. Only about a tenth of the great Sahara desert is sand.

The moving desert

Sandy deserts are always on the move, as wind constantly blows the sand about. The dunes formed by the wind's effect on the sand also change their position, like huge, slow-moving waves.

The expanding desert

Many desert areas are getting bigger. Great expanses of fertile land close to deserts are being destroyed, largely because poor people need to earn a living from the land. They chop down the trees for wood and their goats and other livestock graze the land bare. When droughts occur, the wind blows the bare soil away. Mining and poor farming methods also contribute to the desertification of land.

△ A primitive scoop wheel is used for pumping water in the Nile Valley. These ancient devices, operated by oxen, are still used to irrigate desert land in some parts of the world.

△ Fields and crops on the banks of the Nile show how desert land can be cultivated if water is available.

Reclaiming the land

Governments in many countries are taking steps to prevent more land from becoming desert and to reclaim some of the barren land.

Trees are planted to prevent sand being blown over crops. They also provide firewood and food for domestic animals. In many areas, livestock has been limited. Better farming methods have been introduced, including the rotation of crops, which helps to preserve the soil.

Scientists are continually working on new methods of irrigation (providing water) and developing new varieties of trees and other plants that will grow rapidly in desert soils.

29

Facts and records

The Painted Desert

The Painted Desert is a large area of rocky hills and valleys in northern Arizona, extending about 320 km (200 miles) along the Little Colorado River. It gets its name from the colors and shades of the rocks, which seem to change depending on conditions of heat and light.

△ An aerial view of Ayers Rock, the world's largest monolith.

About 2.5 km (1.5 miles) long, it rises abruptly out of the surrounding plain to a height of 335 m (1,100 ft).

Snow in the desert

Deserts are classified as regions where the average precipitation (fall of water) is less than 25 cm (10 in) a year. But if it is cold enough, this precipitation can fall in the form of snow. It is possible then, for some normally hot deserts to receive the occasional fall of snow.

△ The colorful rocks of the Painted Desert, in Arizona.

Ayers Rock

There are many monoliths (huge, isolated rocks) in the Australian Desert. But one, a giant outcrop of rock called Ayers Rock, stands out above all others. It is the biggest monolith in the world.

△ An unusual sight – part of the Mojave desert, in California, after a fall of snow.

Glossary

Anemometer
An instrument for measuring the speed and direction of the wind.

Aquifer
A layer of rock through which water can flow.

Barren
Not producing any crops or other vegetation.

Butte
A small, flat-topped hill or a small mesa.

Desertification
The changing of non-desert land into desert.

Drought
A period without rain.

Dune
A hill formed by piled-up sand.

Erg
Sandy desert.

Erosion
The wearing away of rock or soil by the action of the weather, running water, ice and wind.

Hammada
A desert with a bare rock surface.

Irrigation
The distribution of water over the land in order to grow crops.

Mesa
A large, flat-topped, steep-sided area, or "table" of rock that stands out from its surroundings.

Oasis
An area in the desert where water is on the surface. The water may be a spring, a well, or a river that flows from nearby mountains across a desert.

Prevailing wind
The wind, noted by direction, that blows most regularly at a particular place.

Reg
Stony or gravely desert.

Rotation of crops
The system of farming in which different crops are grown each year on a piece of land over a number of years. This gets the best use out of the soil.

Seif
Sand dunes that form when two winds blow, the prevailing wind and a wind blowing at rightangles to it.

Index